How to Reach Your Favorite Superstar 2

▼▼▼▼▼

By Dianne J. Woo

LOWELL HOUSE JUVENILE

LOS ANGELES

NTC/Contemporary Publishing Group

Published by Lowell House
A division of NTC/Contemporary Publishing Group, Inc.
4255 West Touhy Avenue, Lincolnwood (Chicago),
Illinois 60712 U.S.A.

Managing Director and Publisher: Jack Artenstein
Director of Publishing Services: Rena Copperman
Editorial Director: Brenda Pope-Ostrow
Director of Art Production: Bret Perry
Project Editor: Amy Downing
Typesetter: Justin Segal
Cover Design: Victor Perry

Lowell House books can be purchased at special discounts
when ordered in bulk for premiums and special sales.
Contact Customer Service at the address above,
or call 1-800-323-4900.

Printed and bound in the United States of America

ISBN: 0-7373-9858-2

OPM 10 9 8 7 6 5 4 3 2 1

Contents

Reach out and get in touch with someone!

Your favorite stars work hard to give you hours of entertainment—and they love to hear that you appreciate their efforts. If you've ever had the impulse to tell a special celeb exactly how you feel, now is the time to do it!

But how do you reach your favorite star? This book will show you how. So read about your favorite celebrities in the following pages, then get out your stationery and write on! And remember these pointers for best results:

➤ If you want a reply, it's best to send a self-addressed, stamped envelope (SASE) along with your letter. That's an envelope that is stamped with the proper postage and has your own name and address printed legibly on it.

➤ If you are writing to or from a country other than the United States, you will need international postage coupons (which are available at any post office). By including the postage coupons, you'll have a better chance of receiving a reply.

➤ Not all celebrities have fan clubs. You might want to request fan club information or, if you feel like you've got the time and devotion, you could ask about setting up a fan club for that star yourself!

➤ Always remember that celebrities change addresses. They move, go on location for months, or change agents. But even if the person you write to decides to move, your letter should be forwarded to the new address.

Have fun! Letter writing is a great way to express yourself to people you care about, and your favorite stars will thank you for being a fan!

Christina Aguilera

□ □

*O*h my God, you guys!" Christina squealed when she won the Grammy. Even as a preschooler, Christina knew she wanted to be a performer. She began at age 5, singing the national anthem at sporting events. At 9, she competed on *Star Search* but lost. Christina didn't give up, and three years later she nabbed a spot on the *Mickey Mouse Club*. That led to her big break: recording "Reflection" for the *Mulan* soundtrack. With her elastic voice and startling range, this daring diva is here to stay.

Birthday Beat
December 18, 1980

So You Want to Know—
How Christina scored the "Reflection" gig? She got the job because she was able to hit a high E. "The note that changed my life," she calls it.

Cool Credits

➤ Grammy, Best New Artist, 2000 ("That was the award I wanted since I was a little girl. When I was 8 or 9, my mom even made me a fake Grammy.")

➤ Her multiplatinum debut album, *Christina Aguilera,* sold more than 250,000 copies in its first week of release.

➤ Hits: "Genie in a Bottle," "What a Girl Wants," "Reflection"

➤ Named one of *Teen People*'s 25 Hottest Stars Under 25

Super Stats

➤ Full name: Christina Maria Aguilera

➤ Birthplace: Staten Island, New York

➤ Raised in: Pittsburgh, Pennsylvania

➤ Family: mother, Shelly, is Irish-American and has played the violin since she was 16; father, Jim, is of Ecuadoran descent and in the military; siblings, Michael, Casey, Rachel, Stephanie

➤ Fave artists: Etta James, No Doubt, Mariah Carey, Whitney Houston

➤ Fave celebs: Johnny Depp, Julio and Enrique Iglesias

➤ Fave sports: baseball, volleyball

➤ Pastimes: shopping, movies, dancing, hanging with her friends

➤ Goals: to get into acting without leaving music; learn Spanish and piano; visit South America

Christina Aguilera
900 S. Alhambra Circle
Coral Gables, FL 33146

Fiona Apple

▼▼▼▼▼▼▼▼▼▼▼▼▼▼▼▼▼▼▼

Super Stats

➤ Birthplace: New York City
➤ Current residence: Los Angeles, California
➤ Family: father, an actor; mother, a former dancer and singer
➤ Fave music: jazz standards
➤ Influences: Billie Holiday, Elton John, Sarah McLachlan
➤ Fave writers: John Irving, Maya Angelou
➤ Dating: writer-director Paul Thomas Anderson, who directed the video of "Fast as You Can," the first single off *When the Pawn…*

Cool Credits

➤ Albums: *Tidal, When the Pawn…*
➤ Hits: "Shadowboxer," "Criminal," "Sleep to Dream," "Fast as You Can"
➤ Grammy, Best Female Rock Vocal Performance (for "Criminal"), 1998
➤ MTV Music Video Award, Best New Artist in a Video (for "Sleep to Dream"), 1997
➤ Performed at Lilith Fair, a tour featuring female artists, 1997

Birthday Beat

September 13, 1977

*I*t's been four years since Fiona exploded out of nowhere with her debut album, *Tidal*. Her tortured songs captured the full range of human emotion and earned her respect and admiration. She took her time before cutting her new album, *When the Pawn...*, writing songs on the road. "In my head I'd play around with certain rhythms, ideas for drum sounds. Generally, I'd think of writing whenever I was overwhelmed by something in my life."

So You Want to Know—

What Fiona's big break was? Her demo got into the hands of a record exec when she baby-sat for the friend of a music insider—right around the time record companies were realizing solo female artists had talent and could make money!

Fiona Apple
509 Hartnell St.
Monterey, CA 93940
or
c/o Sony Music Entertainment
2100 Colorado Ave.
Santa Monica, CA 90404
Official Web site: www.fiona-apple.com

Kobe Bryant

■ ■ ■ ■ ■ ■ ■ ■ ■ ■ ■ ■ ■ ■ ■

From shooting hoops on the courts of Overbrook High School in Philadelphia to playing for the Los Angeles Lakers, Kobe has come a long way in a short time. (By the way, legendary Wilt Chamberlain also first got noticed on the courts of Philly's OHS.) Insiders say he has what it takes to inherit Michael Jordan's throne, but Kobe is content to focus on his game and his exciting, flashy moves. He's no slouch in the rhymin' department, either: He's recorded a rap album, *Visions* (with Tyra Banks), due out in late 2000.

So You Want to Know—

How well Kobe gets along with teammate Shaquille O'Neal? "There's arguments," Kobe has said. "When you have two competitors going head-to-head, something is bound to happen. But as far as our relationship on the court, it's a perfect 10—perfect unison."

Cool Credits

➤ Helped lead the Lakers to win the 2000 NBA championship
➤ Starter for the 1998 All-Star Game, becoming at 19 the youngest all-star in NBA history
➤ NBA All-Rookie Second Team, 1997
➤ Youngest player to start an NBA game, 1997
➤ Won the NBA Slam Dunk Contest, 1997
➤ Selected by the Charlotte Hornets in first round of 1996 NBA draft

Super Stats

➤ Team: Los Angeles Lakers (guard)
➤ Height: 6'7"
➤ Weight: 210

➤ Birthplace: Philadelphia, Pennsylvania
➤ Started playing basketball: age 5
➤ Where his name came from: *Kobe* is a Japanese word for a type of beef.
➤ Family: father, Joe "Jelly Bean" Bryant, a former NBA player; older sisters, Sharia and Shaya
➤ World traveler: lived in Italy as a kid, after his family bought an Italian basketball team—the same team his father played for when he was young
➤ Fave player as a kid: Magic Johnson

Birthday Beat
August 23, 1978

Kobe Bryant
c/o Los Angeles Lakers
3900 W. Manchester Blvd.
P.O. Box 10
Inglewood, CA 90305-2227

B*Witched

🞑 🞑 🞑 🞑 🞑 🞑 🞑 🞑 🞑 🞑 🞑 🞑 🞑 🞑 🞑 🞑 🞑 🞑

*T*his Irish foursome had their humble beginnings in a garage in Dublin. That's where Keavy Lynch was working when she met Sinead O'Carroll, who had brought in her mother's car for repairs. Keavy later met Lindsay Armaou in a kickboxing class, and along with Keavy's twin, Edele, B*Witched was born. They cowrote most of the songs on their first album and are working their magic once again with their second, *Awake and Breathe*. These Celtic soul sisters are out to show the world what girl power is really all about!

Birthday Beat

Keavy and Edele: December 15, 1979
Lindsay: December 18, 1980
Sinead: May 14, 1978

□ □ □ □ □ □ □ □ □ □ □ □ □ □ □ □ □ □ □

Super Stats

➤ Full names: Keavy-Jane Elizabeth Annie Lynch, Edele Claire Christina Edwina Lynch, Lindsay Gael Christina Armaou, Sinead Maria O'Carroll

➤ Birthplaces: Keavy, Edele, and Sinead—Dublin, Ireland; Lindsay—Greece

➤ Current residence: All 4 members live in London.

➤ Family: Edele and Keavy's brother, Shane, is a member of Boyzone.

➤ Secret passion: Sinead—caring for underprivileged kids; Keavy—clean hair

Cool Credits

➤ Albums: *B*Witched, Awake and Breathe*

➤ First act in U.K. history to have their first 4 singles debut at No. 1, beating out the Spice Girls, All Saints, and even the Beatles!

➤ Hits: "C'est la Vie," "Rollercoaster," "Blame It on the Weatherman"

➤ Their first album went platinum in the U.S. and triple platinum in the U.K., selling 3 million copies worldwide.

➤ Opened for *N Sync on their 1999 tour

So You Want to Know—
How B*Witched prepare for a performance? They never go onstage without gathering in an inspirational huddle first.

• • • • • • • • • • • • • • •

B*Witched
c/o Trinity St.
Freepost
3 Alveston Place, Leamington Spa
CV32 4BR
United Kingdom
Official Web site: www.b-witched.com
E-mail: b-witched@b-witched.com

Jennifer Capriati

▼▼▼▼▼▼▼▼▼▼▼▼▼▼▼▼▼▼

*T*en years ago, at age 14, Jennifer was the youngest ever Top 10 player. Then, in the mid-1990s, she hit some hard times and now admits to making the wrong choices. With a new coach, a killer training program, and a new mantra—"Forget the past, live in the now"—she began 2000 by beating No. 5–ranked Mary Pierce and No. 1–ranked Martina Hingis at a Hong Kong exhibition. Then she was a semi-finalist in the Australian Open. By March she was ranked No. 14, up from No. 101 at the start of 1999. This awesome athlete is definitely back on track!

Birthday Beat
March 29, 1976

▼▼▼▼▼▼▼▼▼▼▼▼▼▼▼▼▼▼

So You Want to Know—

How much Jennifer appreciates her fans? While preparing for the 2000 Australian Open, she read about a group of young cancer patients who were tennis fans. She arranged for four of them to come to the tournament as her guests and meet the other competitors.

Cool Credits

➤ Sanex WTA titles: 8
➤ Semifinalist in: Australian Open, 1992, 1993, 2000; Wimbledon, 1991; U.S. Open, 1991; French Open, 1990
➤ Highest singles ranking: No. 6
➤ Grand Slam singles record: 64–25
➤ Gold medalist, 1992 Summer Olympics
➤ At 14, youngest ever Grand Slam semifinalist, French Open, 1990

Super Stats

➤ Height: 5'8½"
➤ Weight: 130
➤ Birthplace: Long Island, New York
➤ Family: father, Stefano; mother, Denise; younger brother, Steven
➤ Turned pro: 1990
➤ Pets: 2 black Labradors, Happy and Aries
➤ Pastimes: reading, writing in her journal, sleeping
➤ Dating: Belgian tennis player Xavier Malisse

Jennifer Capriati
5435 Blue Heron Lane
Wesley Chapel, FL 33543

Jim Carrey

So You Want to Know—

How Jim got the role of the Grinch? Audrey Geisel, the widow of Theodor Geisel (Dr. Seuss), visited the *Man on the Moon* set, where Jim was playing the late comedian Andy Kaufman. Jim, as Andy, did an impression of Jim doing an impression of the Grinch for her! (Got that?)

Cool Credits

➤ Film: *Earth Girls Are Easy; Once Bitten;* two *Ace Ventura* movies; *The Mask; Dumb and Dumber; Batman Forever; The Cable Guy; Liar Liar; The Truman Show; Man on the Moon; Me, Myself & Irene* (with Renée Zellweger). Next up: *Dr. Seuss' How the Grinch Stole Christmas*
➤ TV: *The Duck Factory, Doin' Time on Maple Drive* (TV movie), *In Living Color, Jim Carrey's Unnatural Act* (cable)
➤ Golden Globes, Best Actor in a Drama, *The Truman Show,* 1999, and *Man on the Moon,* 2000

➤ MTV Movie Award, Best Male Performance, 1999

Super Stats

➤ Full name: James Eugene Carrey
➤ Birthplace: Newmarket, Ontario, Canada
➤ Family: daughter, Jane
➤ Difficult times: When Jim was in the 9th grade, his father lost his job, and the entire family ended up homeless for a time.
➤ Began doing standup: age 15, in a Toronto nightclub called Yuk Yuk's

Jim has been making people laugh since he was a kid, when he would put on one-man shows in the basement of his family's home in Canada. By the time he was 19, he was doing standup in L.A. nightclubs. When he was cast in the TV comedy hit *In Living Color,* Jim's ability to create wacky characters by hilariously contorting his body got him the title role in *Ace Ventura, Pet Detective.* Jim was so confident he would be a star that several years ago, he wrote a check to himself for $10 million!

Birthday Beat
January 17, 1962

Jim Carrey
P.O. Box 57593
Sherman Oaks, CA 91403

Vince Carter

□ □ □ □ □ □ □ □ □ □ □ □ □ □ □ □ □

Vince's spectacular dunks—he can "sky" with the best of them—have made him the NBA's fastest rising star. He's been called a slasher who can take his defender right to the basket. In early 2000, Vince was passed over for a spot on the U.S. Olympic Team. He was hurt, but channeled that energy into his game to win the All-Star Slam Dunk Contest. Not long after, he was invited to be on the Olympic Team when Tom Gugliotta of the Phoenix Suns was injured. Vince has accepted, and will soon be on his way to Sydney, Australia.

> **So You Want to Know—**
> What Vince's dunking strategy is? "I'm shying away from dunking on people nowadays because when you try it the second time, it doesn't work.... I have to have a counter, because everybody knows what I can do. Speed can make the difference."

Cool Credits

➤ Leading vote-getter for the All-Star Game, 2000
➤ Won Slam-Dunk Contest at the All-Star Game, 2000
➤ Member, U.S. Olympic Basketball Team, 2000
➤ Helped the Raptors reach the 2000 Eastern Conference playoffs for the first time
➤ NBA Rookie of the Year, 1999
➤ Drafted in 1998 in the first round during his junior year of college

Super Stats

➤ Team: Toronto Raptors (shooting guard)
➤ Height: 6'7"
➤ Weight: 215
➤ Birthplace: Daytona Beach, Florida
➤ Education: University of North Carolina
➤ Mentor: Charles Oakley

Vince Carter
c/o Toronto Raptors
20 Bay St., Ste. 1702
Toronto, Ontario M5J 2N8
Canada

Tom Cruise

▼▼▼▼▼▼▼▼▼▼▼▼▼▼▼▼▼▼▼▼▼

For a bona fide movie star—his films have grossed about $3 billion worldwide—Tom is remarkably unaffected. He loves to talk about films, acting, and his happy marriage to Nicole Kidman. The awkward kid who danced in his underwear in *Risky Business* has matured into a gifted actor with a flair for both serious drama and heart-thumping action. "I like

my job, my life, my family.... I don't know what people really think of me. I mean, I am who I am. 'Tom Cruise' is not a character I play. It's me."

Birthday Beat
July 3, 1962

So You Want to Know—
What was going through Tom's head as he was hanging from that ledge in *M:I-2*? "John [Woo, the director] said, 'Just look at the view. Look at the beauty.' He basically said, 'Look at how awesome this world is.' That's what I'm thinking."

20

Super Stats

➤ Full name: Thomas Cruise Mapother IV
➤ Birthplace: Syracuse, New York
➤ Family: wife, actress Nicole Kidman; daughter, Isabella, 7; son, Connor, 5
➤ Pastimes: sky diving, scuba diving, piloting his Pitts Special S-2B stunt plane
➤ Before Hollywood: played soccer and wrestled at age 17 but gave up both after a knee injury
➤ Fun fact: While he was filming *The Color of Money,* Tom wore an earring for good luck, a diamond given to him by his grandmother.
➤ Fun fact: does all his own stunts, including hanging bare-handed from a 2,000-foot-high cliff in *M:I-2*

Cool Credits

➤ Film highlights: *Taps, The Outsiders, Risky Business, All the Right Moves, Top Gun, The Color of Money, Days of Thunder, Rain Man, Born on the Fourth of July, Far and Away, A Few Good Men, Interview with the Vampire, Jerry Maguire, Mission: Impossible, Eyes Wide Shut, Magnolia, Mission: Impossible 2* (also coproducer). Next up: the sci-fi thriller *Minority Report* (directed by Steven Spielberg)
➤ Academy Award Best Actor nominations, *Born on the Fourth of July* and *Jerry Maguire*; Best Supporting Actor nomination, *Magnolia*
➤ Named one of *People*'s 50 Most Beautiful People in the World, 2000

Tom Cruise
14775 Ventura Blvd., Ste. 1710
Sherman Oaks, CA 91403

Matt Damon

How many young stars today can call themselves a talented actor *and* an Oscar-winning writer to boot? Count cutie Matt Damon among the few. After taking a playwriting course while attending Harvard University, Matt and childhood pal Ben Affleck wrote a draft of what would eventually become the screenplay for *Good Will Hunting*. When the studio wanted bigger-name actors to star in the film, Matt and Ben held out and finally got to star in the roles they had written for themselves—and scored dual Oscars for Best Original Screenplay.

So You Want to Know—

What kind of home Matt lives in? He just moved into a loft in Greenwich Village, New York City. Before that, he lived in hotels. He didn't own a car or even furniture, and carried all his belongings in two duffel bags he bought at Wal-Mart.

Super Stats

➤ Birthplace: Cambridge, Massachusetts
➤ Family: mother, Nancy, a college professor; father, Kent, a real estate agent; brother, Kyle, an artist
➤ Education: studied English at Harvard; dropped out 1 year before graduating to act
➤ First acting job: 1 line in the film *Mystic Pizza*
➤ Big break: a small role in *Courage Under Fire*
➤ Dating: Penélope Cruz, his costar in *All the Pretty Horses*

Cool Credits

➤ Film: *Mystic Pizza, Rising Son* (cable), *School Ties, Geronimo, Courage Under Fire, Good Will Hunting, The Rainmaker, Saving Private Ryan, Rounders, Dogma, The Talented Mr. Ripley, Titan A.E.* (voice-over only), *The Legend of Bagger Vance* (with Will Smith), *All the Pretty Horses*
➤ Academy Award, Best Original Screenplay, *Good Will Hunting,* 1998; also nominated for Best Actor for the same film

Matt Damon
c/o Creative Artists Agency
9830 Wilshire Blvd.
Beverly Hills, CA 90212

Dixie Chicks

Cool Credits

➤ *Wide Open Spaces* is the biggest-selling (6 million plus) debut album by a country group; their second, *Fly,* debuted at No. 1 on the *Billboard* charts.
➤ Grammy Awards, Best Country Performance by a Group (for "Ready to Run") and Best Country Album (*Fly*), 2000
➤ American Music Award, Favorite New Country Artist, 1999
➤ Country Music Awards, Vocal Group of the Year, Single of the Year ("Wide Open Spaces"), and Music Video of the Year ("Wide Open Spaces"), 1998
➤ Only country act to perform at Lilith Fair, a tour featuring female artists

Super Stats

➤ Full names: Martha Elenor Erwin Seidel, Emily Burns Erwin Robison, Natalie Louise Maines
➤ Birthplaces: Martie—York, Pennsylvania; Emily—Dallas, Texas; Natalie—Lubbock, Texas
➤ Pet peeves: Martie—coffee breath; Emily—bad drivers; Natalie—people who chew gum

Birthday Beat

Martie: October 12, 1969
Emily: August 16, 1972
Natalie: October 14, 1974

*T*he Chicks got their start on a street corner in 1989, where sisters Martie and Emily and two others played for tips. Passersby were so impressed, the group started getting professional gigs. Taking their name from the Little Feat song "Dixie Chicken," they opened for such artists as Garth Brooks and Emmylou Harris and performed at the Grand Ole Opry. Natalie joined Martie and Emily in 1995 as lead singer, and together they have made country cool with their spirited three-part harmony and chic style.

So You Want to Know—

Why the Chicks went from jeans and workshirts to little dresses, barrettes, and cardigans? "Natalie said, 'I'll come along and join the band, but I'm not wearing those ugly clothes,'" Martie explains. "Emily and I were kind of relieved because wool gabardine is just not very comfortable or practical in Texas."

Dixie Chicks
56 Lindsley Ave.
Nashville, TN 37210-2039

Omar Epps

Super Stats

➤ Full name: Omar Hashim Epps
➤ Birthplace: Brooklyn, New York
➤ Family: mother, a high school principal; younger sister, Aisha; daughter, Aiyanna
➤ Education: graduated from New York City's High School for the Performing Arts
➤ Loves: silver jewelry
➤ Pastimes: playing basketball, recording rap music, horseback riding
➤ Once roomed with: Marlon Wayans
➤ Dating: Sanaa Lathan, his costar in *The Wood* and *Love & Basketball*

Cool Credits

➤ Film: *Juice, Higher Learning, Major League II, Scream 2, The Mod Squad, In Too Deep, Breakfast of Champions, The Wood, Love & Basketball*
➤ TV: appeared on *The Cosby Show* (as Vanessa Huxtable's first boyfriend); a season of *ER* as Dr. Dennis Gant; the cable films *Daybreak, First Time Felon, Deadly Voyage*
➤ Directed music videos for Heather B, Special Ed, and his own rap duo, Wolfpack

Birthday Beat
July 23, 1973

One look into Omar's honest, soulful eyes and you can see why he's one of Hollywood's hottest young stars. With solid supporting roles in *The Wood* and *Scream 2*, he was turning heads even before he snagged his first leading role as Quincy in *Love & Basketball.* He just formed his own production company, BKNY, to produce a script he's written, *Who Stole the Soul,* about a hip-hop star. This so-fine actor certainly will be stealing hearts for years to come.

So You Want to Know—

What it was like working with Sanaa on *Love & Basketball*? He didn't treat her any differently in the ball-playing scenes because she's a girl. "I don't discriminate.... You come on the court with me and you're gonna get it like one of the boys...and she did not want me stopping a take to go, 'Oh, baby, did you stub your toe?'"

Omar Epps
9701 Wilshire Blvd., 10th Floor
Beverly Hills, CA 90212

Nomar Garciaparra

*I*n Nomar's first season, he set a
record for most homers by a rookie
shortstop, and ended with a .306 average and 98 RBIs. That led to his being
unanimously voted the American League
Rookie of the Year. He ended his second
season with a .323 average and 119 RBIs.
In 1999, he overcame a series of injuries to
win his first AL batting title. Nomar's batting and fielding skills are phenomenal,
and many consider him the best player in
the game today.

Birthday Beat
July 23, 1973

■ ■ ■ ■ ■ ■ ■ ■ ■ ■ ■ ■ ■ ■ ■ ■ ■

So You Want to Know—

What's behind all those habits of his: tugging his batting glove, tapping his shoe, spitting into his glove? Nomar says they're just routines. "It's important to be comfortable out there. Having a routine makes me comfortable."

Super Stats

➤ Team: Boston Red Sox (shortstop)
➤ Full name: Anthony Nomar Garciaparra ("Nomar" is his father's name, Ramon, spelled backward.)
➤ Height: 6'0"
➤ Weight: 185
➤ Birthplace: Whittier, California
➤ Education: attended Georgia Tech
➤ Nickname: Spider-Man, for his outstanding fielding skills
➤ Digs: the U.S. Women's Soccer Team

Cool Credits

➤ Drafted in first round by the Red Sox in 1994
➤ First Major Leaguer since Mark McGwire (and the fifth in history) to hit 30-plus home runs in his first 2 seasons
➤ AL Batting Crown, 1999
➤ All-Star, 1997, 1999
➤ Silver Slugger Award, 1997
➤ ESPY Breakthrough Player of the Year, 1997
➤ AL Rookie of the Year, 1997
➤ Member, U.S. Olympic Baseball Team, 1992

• •

Nomar Garciaparra
c/o Boston Red Sox
4 Yawkey Way
Boston, MA 02215-3496

• •

Jeff Gordon

□ □ □ □ □ □ □ □ □ □ □ □ □ □ □ □ □ □

One of the hottest drivers on the NASCAR circuit today—and one of the most popular—Jeff got behind the wheel at the tender age of 5. In 1979, 8-year-old Jeff was the Quarter-Midget National Champion. By 24, he was the youngest points champion of the modern era. His 1998 win in the Brickyard 400 earned him the No. 2 spot on the all-time money-winners list. In his short career, Jeff has earned more than $31 million!

So You Want to Know—

Besides his car and his racing team, what is the key to all of Jeff's wins? He is incredibly superstitious. He doesn't allow anyone on his team to wear green, and he won't let them eat peanuts because he thinks they're bad luck.

Super Stats

➤ Height: 5'7"
➤ Weight: 150
➤ Birthplace: Pittsboro, Indiana
➤ Family: wife, Brooke
➤ Pastimes: waterskiing, snow skiing, racquetball, video games

Cool Credits

➤ Second youngest driver in history to win the NASCAR Winston Cup Series Championship, and the youngest to win 3 championships, 1995, 1997, 1998
➤ Finished sixth in the point standings, 1999
➤ Second driver ever to win the Winston Million
➤ Won Brickyard 400, 1994, 1998
➤ Won Daytona 500, 1997
➤ American Driver of the Year, 1995
➤ Winston Cup Rookie of the Year, 1993
➤ Won Midget Championship, 1990

Birthday Beat

August 4, 1971

Jeff Gordon
c/o Jeff Gordon National Fan Club
P.O. Box 515
Williams, AZ 86046-0515
Official Web site: www.jeffgordon.com

Macy Gray

As soon as you hear that unmistakable voice, you know it's Macy. She can sound sweet on one song, raspy on the next. Macy got her start when she hooked up with some musician friends in L.A. She wrote lyrics for them just for fun, and they asked Macy to fill in for the lead singer. When the tape got around, the calls started coming in. She signed a record deal in 1998, and two months later began work on her first album. Macy writes from the heart and has created her own unique blend of soul, hip-hop, R&B, funk, and rock.

Super Stats

➤ Birthplace: Canton, Ohio
➤ Musical training: 7 years of classical piano lessons, starting at age 7
➤ Background: grew up on a variety of music—thanks to her parents' vast record collection—including R&B, hip-hop, and rock ("I developed a real appreciation for all kinds of music just by being exposed to it.")

So You Want to Know—

If Macy Gray is her real name? No. Macy Gray was a friend of her dad's who lived next door. "Everybody always called him by his whole name, like they'd say, 'MacyGray is outside,' or 'Where's MacyGray?' So his name always stuck with me.… I have a long, drawn-out Midwestern name. If I used my real name, you wouldn't be wanting to talk to me," she jokes.

➤ Education: studied screenwriting at USC
➤ Opened her own club, The We Ours, where she rehearses her act and chills with her friends

Birthday Beat
December 6, 1969

Cool Credits

➤ Debut album, *On How Life Is,* released in 1999, went double platinum
➤ Brit Awards (the British version of the Grammys) for Best International Solo Artist, Female, and Best International Newcomer, 2000
➤ Grammy nominations, Best R&B Female Vocal Performance (for "Do Something") and Best New Artist, 2000

Macy Gray
c/o Sony Music Entertainment
2100 Colorado Ave.
Santa Monica, CA 90404
Official Web site: www.macygray.com

Mia Hamm

So You Want to Know—

How sports shaped Mia as a person? "Sports were a way for me to fit in.... I'm not a real extrovert, and I was usually in the background. So it was easier for me to communicate with people through sports."

Cool Credits

➤ Only athlete to be named U.S. Soccer Athlete of the Year 5 years in a row, 1994, 1995, 1996, 1997, 1998

➤ Holds first place for all-time in career goals with her 108th goal on May 22, 1999, against Brazil in a 3–0 victory

➤ ESPY Award, Outstanding Female Athlete, 1998

➤ MVP, Women's World Cup, 1995, 1997

➤ Led U.S. Women's Team to Olympic gold medal, 1996

➤ NCAA Player of the Year, 1990, 1992, 1993

➤ At 15, youngest player ever on the National Team

Super Stats

➤ Team: U.S. Women's Soccer (forward)

➤ Full name: Mariel Margret Hamm

➤ Height: 5'5"

➤ Weight: 125

➤ Birthplace: Selma, Alabama

➤ Family: father, a pilot; mother, a ballerina; 5 siblings; husband, Marine Corps pilot Christian Corry

➤ Education: graduated in 1994 from the University of North Carolina with a degree in political science

➤ Started the Mia Hamm Foundation to fund research for bone marrow diseases and to encourage and empower young female athletes

*C*onsidered the best all-around female soccer player in the world, Mia has undoubtedly contributed to the increasing popularity of women's soccer. She helped lead the U.S. Women's Soccer Team to a memorable victory in the 1999 Women's World Cup, and she is working hard to establish a professional women's soccer league. Mia has more than earned her reputation as "soccer's deadliest weapon."

Birthday Beat
March 17, 1972

Mia Hamm
U.S. Soccer Federation
1801 S. Prairie Ave.
Chicago, IL 60616

Melissa Joan Hart

Cool Credits

➤ Made her directorial debut with the January 21, 2000, episode of *Sabrina*
➤ Film: *Can't Hardly Wait, Drive Me Crazy*
➤ TV: *Sabrina the Teenage Witch; Clarissa Explains It All* (cable); appeared on *Touched by an Angel* and the TV movies *Silencing Mary* and *Christmas Snow*
➤ Stage: *The Crucible, Beside Herself, Imagining Brad*
➤ Received a CableAce nomination for *Clarissa Explains It All*

Super Stats

➤ Birthplace: Sayville, New York
➤ Current residence: Los Angeles, California

➤ Family: mother, Paula, who is her manager and executive producer of *Sabrina*; father, William, a shellfish wholesaler; 5 sisters, 1 brother (all are actors except one, who is a producer); 2 half sisters
➤ Family business: Melissa and her mother are partners in Hartbreak Films, which produces the *Sabrina* series and TV movies, as well as the *Sabrina* Saturday morning cartoon featuring the voice of Melissa's sister Emily.
➤ Charities: Starlight Children's Foundation, Pediatric AIDS/Kids for Kids, Earthjustice (a nonprofit law firm for the environment)

So You Want to Know—

When Melissa was bitten by the acting bug? At age 4, she begged her mother to take her to a *Romper Room* audition. She didn't get the job, but she did begin auditioning for commercials. She appeared in 22 commercials that year!

*S*he's been riding high as spunky teen witch Sabrina Spellman for the past four years, but Melissa is remarkably down to earth, thanks to her close family ties. When Melissa was a child, her mother, Paula, would drive the entire Hart clan—seven children in all—into New York City for auditions. In 2000, Melissa landed her first starring role in a feature film, *Drive Me Crazy*. "The more you put into anything, the more you get out of it," she has said. "If you put time and energy into something, good is bound to come out of it."

Birthday Beat
April 18, 1976

Melissa Joan Hart
10880 Wilshire Blvd., Ste. 1101
Los Angeles, CA 90024-4101

Dominik Hasek

▼▼▼▼▼▼▼▼▼▼▼▼▼▼▼▼▼▼▼

With his strength, speed, rebound control, and intense concentration, no wonder Dominik has five Vezina trophies and two Hart trophies (given to the league MVP) on his mantel. Chalk it up to this goalie's unusual style—in a clinch, he'll often drop his stick and grab the puck with his blocker hand. When Dominik led the Czech team to a gold medal in the 1998 Olympics, he was given a hero's welcome back home in Prague: 700,000 fans greeted the team at the airport.

38

Cool Credits

➤ NHL All-Star, 1993, 1994, 1995, 1996, 1997, 1998
➤ Vezina trophy winner, 1994, 1995, 1997, 1998, 1999
➤ Hart trophy winner, 1997, 1998
➤ Gold medal, 1998 Olympics
➤ First goaltender since George Hainsworth to record 6 shutouts in 1 month (December 1997)
➤ Drafted by thc Chicago Blackhawks, 1988; joined Sabres, 1992

Super Stats

➤ Team: Buffalo Sabres (goalie)
➤ Height: 5'11"
➤ Weight: 168
➤ Birthplace: Pardubice, Czech Republic
➤ Nickname: the Dominator
➤ Fave food: pizza
➤ Fave player: Jaromir Jagr

So You Want to Know—

How much the Czech Republic loves Dominik? When a world-famous astronomer discovered a huge comet more than 240 million miles away from Earth, he named it the Dominik Hasek Comet.

Dominik Hasek
c/o Buffalo Sabres
Marine Midland Arena
One Seymour H. Knox III Plaza
Buffalo, NY 14203

Jennifer Love Hewitt

■ ■ ■ ■ ■ ■ ■ ■ ■ ■ ■ ■ ■

No stranger to stage and screen, Jennifer was born to perform. When she was 3 years old, she managed to sneak away from her mom at a dinner club and soon was onstage singing! Within two years, she had already started dance lessons, and by the time she was 10, she was traveling around the world, performing in front of large audiences. Her secret? When she's working, she devotes "250,000 percent" to everything she does.

So You Want to Know—

How Jennifer handles the ups and downs of show business? "There have been tons of things that I really wanted, movies that I lost out for because I was too short or didn't have the right color hair. But I try to turn those negatives into positives and go, 'But wow, look what I have been given in my life.'"

Cool Credits

➤ TV: *Kids Incorporated, Shaky Ground, The Byrds of Paradise, Little Miss Millions* (cable), *Party of Five, Time of Your Life, The Audrey Hepburn Story* (TV movie)
➤ Film: *Munchies, Sister Act 2: Back in the Habit, House Arrest, Can't Hardly Wait, The Suburbans, I Know What You Did Last Summer* and its sequel. Next up: the crime comedy *Breakers* (with Sigourney Weaver); tentatively set to play an FBI agent in *Trust Me*
➤ Albums: *Love Songs, Let's Go Bang, Jennifer Love Hewitt*
➤ Named one of *Teen People*'s 25 Hottest Stars Under 25

Super Stats

➤ Birthplace: Waco, Texas
➤ Nickname: Love
➤ Best friend: her mom, Pat
➤ Pet: a cat named Don Juan
➤ Fave foods: strawberries with whipped cream, mushroom pizza, chocolate
➤ Fave artists: Smash Mouth, Third Eye Blind, Matchbox 20, Backstreet Boys
➤ Production company: owns Love Spell Entertainment, which has 4 feature films in development

Birthday Beat
February 21, 1979

Jennifer Love Hewitt
c/o William Morris Agency
151 El Camino Dr.
Beverly Hills, CA 90212-2775

Enrique Iglesias

□ □ □ □ □ □ □ □ □ □ □ □ □ □ □ □ □ □ □ □

*I*f anyone rivals Ricky Martin for the title of Hottest Mambo King, it's Enrique. Sure, he may have a famous father, the legendary Julio Iglesias, but Enrique has made a name for himself on his own. He used to turn in demo tapes under a different name so people would hire him for his singing talent instead of his background. That tactic paid off, and now he's riding high in the U.S. and worldwide, doing what he loves most: creating music.

So You Want to Know—

How Enrique feels about his fans? "I think it's better to get attention than to *not* get attention. The day I've got to worry is the day that I go out there and nobody makes a big scene or asks me for an autograph or a picture. If it wasn't for those people, I wouldn't be here."

Super Stats

➤ Birthplace: Madrid, Spain
➤ Current residence: Miami, Florida
➤ Pet: Grammy, a golden retriever given to him by his record label after he won the award
➤ Inspirations: the Rolling Stones, the Police, Dire Straits
➤ Pastimes: waterskiing, scuba diving, watching Road Runner cartoons
➤ What he looks for in a girl: "Talent. If she's a great singer or dancer, that for me is the biggest turn-on."

Cool Credits

➤ *Billboard* Hot Latin Tracks Artist of the Year, 2000
➤ Before his English-language debut album, *Enrique* (featuring the hit single "Bailamos"), was released in the U.S. in 1999, his 3 previous Spanish-language albums had sold 14 million worldwide.
➤ Named one of *Teen People*'s 25 Hottest Stars Under 25
➤ Grammy Award, Best Latin Pop Album, 1996

Birthday Beat
May 8, 1975

Enrique Iglesias
c/o Interscope Records
10900 Wilshire Blvd., #1230
Los Angeles, CA 90024

Jaromir Jagr

▼▼▼▼▼▼▼▼▼▼▼▼▼▼▼▼▼

*S*ince 1991, Jaromir has matured from an outstanding rookie into an accomplished, powerful member of the Pittsburgh Penguins and a force to be reckoned with. In 1999, he won not only the Hart trophy for Most Valuable Player, but also the Art Ross trophy and Lester B. Pearson Award for MVP. He is only the second player in team history (after Mario Lemieux) to win all three of these awards in one year.

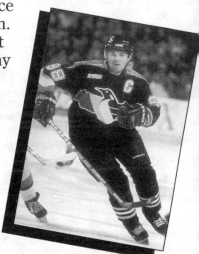

Super Stats

➤ Team: Pittsburgh Penguins (right wing)
➤ Birthplace: Kladno, Czech Republic
➤ Height: 6'2"
➤ Weight: 228
➤ Shoots: left
➤ NHL debut: October 5, 1990, against Washington Capitals

Birthday Beat

February 15, 1972

Cool Credits

➤ Won the Hart trophy, 1999
➤ Won the Art Ross trophy, 1995, 1998, 1999
➤ Lester B. Pearson Award, 1999
➤ NHL First Team All-Star, 1999, his fourth selection in the last 5 years
➤ Led the league in assists (83) and power-play assists (34), 1999
➤ Only NHL player to record 100 points, 1998
➤ Drafted by the Penguins in first round (fifth overall), 1990

So You Want to Know—

What kind of rookie year Jaromir had? For starters, he was the first Czech player to attend the draft without having to defect. He led all rookies in the playoffs with 13 points and 10 assists. He set an NHL record for the most assists (5) by a rookie in the Stanley Cup Finals. Finally, he was named to the NHL All-Star Rookie Team.

Jaromir Jagr
c/o Pittsburgh Penguins
Civic Arena
Gate 9
Pittsburgh, PA 15219
Official Web site: www.nhlpenguins.com

Angelina Jolie

From a gangster's moll in *Playing God* to a rookie cop in *The Bone Collector,* Angelina shines in her portrayals of edgy characters. She made a name for herself in the cable film *Gia,* which earned her a Golden Globe and a Screen Actors Guild Award. Since then she's been on the fast track to stardom, and the awards keep coming in—she nabbed both an Oscar and a Golden Globe for playing a mental patient in *Girl, Interrupted*. It's in her genes—Angelina's parents are both actors.

So You Want to Know—

How Angelina is handling her newfound fame? "I'm pretty grounded, but I'm scared of celebrity. Because as much as I'm kind of out there, I'm really an observer. I like to watch people. And you can't be an observer if you're famous."

Cool Credits

➤ Film: *Hackers; Playing God; Playing by Heart; Pushing Tin; The Bone Collector; Girl, Interrupted; Gone in 60 Seconds*. Next up: the thriller *Dancing in the Dark* (with Antonio Banderas)
➤ Cable: *Gia, Wallace, True Women*
➤ Appeared in music videos for the Rolling Stones and Lenny Kravitz
➤ Golden Globe and Academy Award, Best Supporting Actress, *Girl, Interrupted,* 2000
➤ Golden Globe and Screen Actors Guild Award, Best Actress, *Gia,* 1999
➤ Golden Globe for *Wallace,* 1998
➤ Named one of *Teen Movieline*'s 20 Best Actors 25 and Under

Super Stats

➤ Full name: Angelina Jolie Voight
➤ Birthplace: Los Angeles, California
➤ Current residence: New York City
➤ Family: father, Oscar-winning actor Jon Voight; mother, French actress Marcheline Bertrand; brother, James Haven
➤ Love: married actor-writer-director Billy Bob Thornton (her costar in *Pushing Tin*) in May 2000
➤ Fun fact: *Angelina Jolie* means "pretty little angel" in French.
➤ Film debut: appeared opposite her father in 1982's *Lookin' to Get Out*

Birthday Beat
June 4, 1975

Angelina Jolie
c/o William Morris Agency
151 El Camino Dr.
Beverly Hills, CA 90212-2775

Cobi Jones

C obi left UCLA during his junior year to try out for the national soccer team—and made it, of course. One of the fastest players in the league, he has racked up 126 caps since his 1992 National Team debut against the Ivory Coast. He played with clubs in Brazil and England before joining the Galaxy. With the Galaxy, he scored the team's first goal in the 37th minute of their opening-day victory over the New York–New Jersey MetroStars in 1996.

Birthday Beat
June 16, 1970

□ [

Super Stats

➤ Team: Los Angeles Galaxy (forward/midfielder)
➤ Full name: Cobi N'gai Jones
➤ Height: 5'7"
➤ Weight: 145
➤ Birthplace: Detroit, Michigan
➤ Grew up in: Westlake Village, California
➤ Family: parents, Freeman and Mada; brothers, Freeman and Bruce; sister, Kerry
➤ Goal: to become a lawyer

Cool Credits

➤ Played all matches in both World Cup 1994 and World Cup 1998
➤ Chevrolet/U.S. Soccer Male Athlete of the Year, 1998
➤ Copa America Tournament, 1995
➤ Tied for all-time assist leader (11) in U.S. National Team history
➤ Gold medal, Pan American Games, 1991
➤ NSCAA All-American, 1991
➤ TV: appeared on *Beverly Hills, 90210*

So You Want to Know—

How Cobi got his eye on the ball? He started playing soccer as a kid because a cousin of his played. In 1988, Cobi was the top-scoring freshman at UCLA, and in his junior year, he helped UCLA win the national title.

• •

Cobi Jones
c/o Los Angeles Galaxy
1640 S. Sepulveda Blvd., Ste. 114
Los Angeles, CA 90025

49

• •

Heidi Klum

With her gorgeous face and athletic body, this supermodel rules the runways. Heidi's expression can be cool and confident one moment, romantic and fragile the next. At home in Germany when she was 18, Heidi and a friend were casually flipping through a magazine when they spotted an ad for a modeling competition. Heidi was reluctant at first, but her friend eventually persuaded her to enter. Heidi's victory in the contest led to a three-year contract with a top New York agency, and she modeled in Paris, Milan, and Tokyo before making her mark in the U.S.

Cool Credits

➤ Victoria's Secret catalog, *GQ, Sports Illustrated*'s 1999 Swimsuit Issue (cover)
➤ TV: 3 episodes of *Spin City* as Michael J. Fox's love interest

Super Stats

➤ Height: 5'9½"
➤ Birthplace: Cologne, Germany
➤ Current residence: New York City
➤ Eyes: hazel
➤ Hair: brown
➤ Dislikes: flying
➤ Agency: Metropolitan

So You Want to Know—

What Heidi made sure she had before entering the jet-setting world of modeling? Three things: a lawyer, a worldwide insurance policy, and a cellular phone so she could call her parents anywhere, anytime.

Heidi Klum
c/o IMG Models
304 Park Ave. South, Penthouse North
New York, NY 10010

Jude Law

*L*uscious Jude Law, a talented, classically trained actor, has been called the perfect specimen of male beauty. After appearing in several British films, he landed his first two American movies, *Gattaca* and *Midnight in the Garden of Good and Evil.* Now, after being Oscar-nominated for *The Talented Mr. Ripley,* this Jude is no longer obscure—he's on his way to becoming a major star. "I'll go anywhere, play any role, if the part speaks to me or the story has something new to say."

So You Want to Know—

How Jude prepared for his role as a paraplegic in *Gattaca*? He stopped walking altogether and would literally crawl up the stairs to his apartment. He was so convincing that after the film was finished, the director saw a picture of Jude standing up and didn't recognize him!

Super Stats

➤ Birthplace and current residence: London

➤ Name origin: Jude comes from the Beatles song "Hey Jude" and also the title character in Thomas Hardy's classic novel *Jude the Obscure*.

➤ Family: wife, actress Sadie Frost; son, Rafferty, 3; stepson, Finlay, 9; parents, Maggie and Peter, both retired teachers; sister, Natasha

➤ On the birth of his son: "I think it gave me a very vital and grounding ingredient to being an actor. It broke my sleeping pattern, that's for sure."

➤ Fave childhood book: *Animal Farm*

➤ Pastime: yoga

Cool Credits

➤ Stage: *Pygmalion, The Fastest Clock in the Universe, The Snow Orchid, Death of a Salesman, Indiscretions*; also performed with the Royal Shakespeare Company and Britain's National Theatre

➤ Film: *Shopping, Wilde, Bent, Gattaca, Midnight in the Garden of Good and Evil, Music from Another Room, eXistenZ, The Talented Mr. Ripley, The Wisdom of Crocodiles*

➤ Nominated for a Best Supporting Actor Academy Award for *The Talented Mr. Ripley*

➤ Named one of *People*'s 50 Most Beautiful People in the World, 2000

➤ Won a Theatre World Award and received a Tony nomination for *Indiscretions*, 1995

Jude Law
13 Shorts Garden
London SC2H 9AT
England

Tobey Maguire

□ □ □ □ □ □ □ □ □ □ □ □ □ □ □ □ □ □ □

With his sincere, soulful blue eyes, Tobey brings both a childlike innocence and an adult wisdom to the young dreamers he often plays. After his parents divorced when he was a kid, Tobey shuffled between schools until acting classes gave him the structure

and stability he needed. His big break came when he appeared in a short film called *Duke of Groove,* which got him cast in *The Ice Storm,* and Hollywood took note of his potential star quality.

Birthday Beat
June 27, 1975

54

Cool Credits

➤ Film: *Deconstructing Harry, Fear and Loathing in Las Vegas, Joyride, This Boy's Life, The Ice Storm, Pleasantville, Ride with the Devil, The Cider House Rules, Wonder Boys*

➤ TV: *Great Scott!*, *Tracey Takes On…*, the TV movies *Spoils of War* and *A Child's Cry for Help*
➤ Named one of *Teen Movieline*'s 20 Best Actors 25 and Under

So You Want to Know—

What the turning point in his career was? At a rehearsal when he was 16, the director asked Tobey to sing like a mouse, then like an ox. "I had to commit myself 100 percent even to get through it, and it was that commitment…that made me realize growth is endless within this job: that I can always be scared and challenge myself."

Super Stats

➤ Full name: Tobias Vincent Maguire
➤ Birthplace: Inglewood, California
➤ Current residence: Los Angeles, California
➤ Family: father, a chef; mother, Wendy, a secretary
➤ Friends: Leonardo DiCaprio, Lukas Haas, Jay Ferguson
➤ Fave artists: Beck, the Beastie Boys, the Cure, Led Zeppelin
➤ Pastimes: yoga, cooking, video games
➤ Dislikes: his name, because he says it sounds like something you'd call a dog
➤ Fun fact: Tobey wanted to be a chef like his father, but his mother paid him $100 to take drama classes instead of home economics.

Tobey Maguire
955 S. Carrillo Dr., Ste. 300
Los Angeles, CA 90048

Peyton Manning

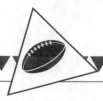

So You Want to Know—

What Peyton attributes his success to? His parents' love and support, and the confidence sports gives him, have kept him on the straight and narrow. Peyton believes that if kids have something to care about—like sports—they have more self-worth and are less willing to do something self-destructive.

Super Stats

➤ Team: Indianapolis Colts (quarterback)
➤ Height: 6'5"
➤ Weight: 230
➤ Birthplace and current residence: New Orleans, Louisiana
➤ Education: University of Tennessee, where he holds virtually every passing record and is working on a master's degree in sports management
➤ Family: father is former New Orleans Saints quarterback Archie Manning

➤ Charities: Special Olympics Louisiana; CASA (Court Appointed Special Advocates), a children's services organization

Cool Credits

➤ Pro Bowl, 1999
➤ Set Colts and NFL records in completions, attempts, yards, touchdowns, and consecutive games with a touchdown pass (13), 1998
➤ Selected by the Colts with the first pick in the NFL draft, 1998
➤ Runner-up for the Heisman trophy, 1997
➤ NCAA All-American, 1996, 1997

When the Indianapolis Colts picked Peyton with the first selection in the 1998 draft, he embarked on a successful, record-setting year and has been compared with John Elway, Steve Young, and Brett Favre. But this quarterback hasn't forgotten his roots: He gives back to the community by reading stories to schoolkids, making personal appearances for charity, and being a good role model.

Birthday Beat
March 24, 1976

Peyton Manning
c/o Indianapolis Colts
P.O. Box 535000
Indianapolis, IN 46253
Official Web site: www.peytonmanning.com

Ricky Martin

He burst onto the U.S. music scene with his hip-shaking, eye-popping performance of "La Copa de la Vida" (The Cup of Life) at the 1999 Grammy Awards. Since then, fans can't get enough of Ricky. He's caused traffic jams in New York City and sold out concert after concert. Through it all, Ricky has a driving ambition to shatter the stereotypes of Latinos—particularly Puerto Ricans like himself. "Whatever it is that I have to do to unite Puerto Rico or Latin America with the rest of the world, well, let's go for it."

So You Want to Know—

Would Ricky ever give up performing? He says music is a way of life and wants to keep doing it until the day he dies. But if he ever gets tired of singing, he has no problem moving on to something else.

Cool Credits

➤ His debut English-language album, *Ricky Martin,* has sold more than 6 million copies.
➤ Named one of *People*'s 50 Most Beautiful People in the World, 2000
➤ Grammy Award, Best Latin Pop Performance (for *Vuelve*), 1999
➤ Won Best Dance and Best Pop at the 1999 MTV Video Awards
➤ *Entertainment Weekly*'s Entertainer of the Year, 1999
➤ Film: He's being considered to star in the sequel to *Dirty Dancing.*
➤ TV: Miguel on *General Hospital*
➤ Stage: *Les Misérables*

Super Stats

➤ Full name: Enrique Martin Morales
➤ Birthplace: Hato Rey, Puerto Rico
➤ Childhood name: Kiki
➤ Family: father, Enrique, a psychologist; mother, Nereida Morales, an accountant; 5 siblings
➤ Pastimes: yoga, rock climbing, going to the gym, meditating
➤ Insecurity: his derriere ("It's tiny. What can I do?")

Birthday Beat
December 24, 1971

Ricky Martin
3720 Canterbury Way
Boca Raton, FL 33434

Dylan McDermott

*O*nscreen, cool, magnetic Dylan McDermott projects both strength and vulnerability. But Dylan's life has not always been easy. When he was 5, his parents split up, and his mother died from an accidental gunshot wound shortly after. "It shapes you forever, and you don't get over it," he has said. "It was either going to kill me or make me stronger." Raised by his grandmother, Dylan pursued acting and eventually landed the plum role of criminal defense attorney Bobby Donnell on TV's award-winning *The Practice*.

So You Want to Know—
How Dylan got that dashing smile of his? "I was in a car wreck and my teeth hit the dashboard. They went a little crooked."

Cool Credits

➤ Film: *Steel Magnolias, In the Line of Fire, Hamburger Hill, The Cowboy Way, Blue Iguana, Home for the Holidays, Destiny Turns on the Radio, 'Til There Was You, Playing by Heart, Three to Tango, Texas Rangers*
➤ TV: *The Practice*; hosted VH1's *100 Greatest Songs of Rock & Roll*
➤ Stage: *Biloxi Blues, Golden Boy*
➤ Named one of *People*'s 50 Most Beautiful People in the World, 2000
➤ Named one of *GQ*'s 1999 Men of the Year
➤ Golden Globe, Best Actor in a TV Drama, *The Practice*, 1998
➤ Drama-Logue Award for the play *Short Eyes*, 1994, which also marked his directorial debut

Super Stats

➤ Birthplace: Waterbury, Connecticut
➤ Current residence: Brentwood, California
➤ Family: wife, actress Shiva Afshar; daughter, Colette, age 4; father, Richard; mother, Diane; maternal grandmother, Avis Marino; sister, Robin
➤ Mentor: actress-director Joanne Woodward
➤ Talent: plays the violin
➤ Fave pastimes: basketball, renovating the family home, watching *Rugrats* with daughter Colette
➤ Fun fact: often gave animals to his ex-girlfriends; Julia Roberts got a basset hound

Birthday Beat

October 26, 1962

Dylan McDermott
P.O. Box 25516
Los Angeles, CA 90025-0516

Monica

▼▼▼▼▼▼▼▼▼▼▼▼▼▼▼▼▼▼▼▼▼▼

B ehind that rock-the-house voice, Monica is a confident and intelligent artist. She began singing in the church choir at age 4, and by the time she was 12 she'd won more than 20 talent contests. A record exec brought her to New York, and at 14 she cut her first single. After a yearlong promotional tour, she graduated from high school with a 4.0 GPA. Other young pop stars may come and go, but Monica has the raw talent and maturity to stay in the spotlight.

Birthday Beat
October 24, 1980

So You Want to Know—
Is there a rivalry with Brandy? Monica quickly lays those rumors to rest. "We have an extremely incredible business relationship.... We are 'friendly.' We don't dislike each other."

Cool Credits

➤ Albums: *Miss Thang, The Boy Is Mine*
➤ Hit singles: "Angel of Mine," "This Boy Is Mine" (duet with Brandy), "For You I Will" (from *Space Jam*), "Why I Love You So Much"
➤ At 14, was the youngest performer ever to have 2 consecutive No. 1 hits ("Don't Take It Personal" and "Before You Walk Out of My Life") on the *Billboard* R&B singles chart
➤ *Billboard* Artist of the Year, 1996

Super Stats

➤ Full name: Monica Arnold
➤ Birthplace: College Park (outside Atlanta), Georgia
➤ Family: mother, Marilyn; stepfather, the Rev. Edward Best; younger brother, Montez; cousin Melinda Dancil, her manager
➤ Fave foods: crab legs and collard greens
➤ What she looks for in a guy: someone who's interesting, focused, understanding, and not into games
➤ Inspirations: Whitney Houston, Aretha Franklin, Rachelle Farrell

Monica
c/o Arista Records
9975 Santa Monica Blvd., 2nd Floor
Beverly Hills, CA 90212
or
c/o Monica Fan Club
P.O. Box 672557
Marietta, GA 30006-0056
E-mail: monica.a@endoramail.com

Randy Moss

Not long after he was the Minnesota Vikings' first-round pick in 1998, Randy took the NFL by storm, setting a new league record for most touchdown receptions (17) by a rookie. He also was the only rookie in 1998 to earn a spot in the 1999 Pro Bowl, where he was a starter. Many football insiders say that Randy is well on his way to becoming one of the greatest players ever in the game.

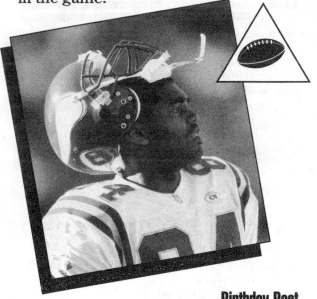

Birthday Beat
February 13, 1977

Cool Credits

➤ Pro Bowl, 1999, 2000
➤ MVP, 50th Annual Pro Bowl
➤ Associated Press NFL All-Pro Team, 1999
➤ Drafted by the Vikings in the first round, 1998
➤ Offensive Rookie of the Year, 1998
➤ NFL Alumni Wide Receiver of the Year, 1998
➤ Heisman trophy finalist, 1997
➤ Mid-American Conference Player of the Year, 1997
➤ State Football Player of the Year (senior year in high school)

Super Stats

➤ Team: Minnesota Vikings (wide receiver)
➤ Height: 6'4"
➤ Weight: 198
➤ Birthplace: Rand, West Virginia
➤ Education: Marshall College, where he had a 53-touchdown career

---

So You Want to Know—

Besides pro ball, what other goals does Randy have? "Part of my dream is to give back to the one person who's done everything for me—my mom. She's worked hard and raised three kids by herself, and I don't want to risk not being able to take care of her."

Randy Moss
c/o Minnesota Vikings
9520 Viking Dr.
Eden Prairie, MN 55344

*N Sync

□ □ □ □ □ □ □ □

In 1998, *N Sync rocketed to fame with their first album, and these five gorgeous guys don't show any signs of slowing down. Their follow-up, *No Strings Attached,* sold 1.1 million copies in just the first 24 hours, and their 2000 tour sold a record-setting 1 million tickets the first day! The band's energetic mix of pop and R&B definitely has fans hankering for more—and with J.C., Joey, Chris, Lance, and Justin venturing into TV and movies, they won't be disappointed!

So You Want to Know—

What has been the highlight of the band's success? "We got to hang out with the president," J.C. says. "We watched *Music of the Heart* in his private theater at the White House." Lance adds, "We were throwing popcorn at everybody.... [Bill Clinton] wouldn't participate, but it was such a blast."

Cool Credits

➤ First album, **N Sync,* went platinum; second album, *No Strings Attached,* sold 2.4 million copies the first week
➤ Hit single "Bye Bye Bye" from *No Strings Attached* broke the Backstreet Boys' record for most additions to radio playlists across the U.S.
➤ Book: **Nside *Nsync*
➤ Justin, J.C., and Lance were named three of *Teen People*'s 25 Hottest Stars Under 25

Super Stats

➤ Full names: J.C.— Joshua Scott Chasez; Joey—Joseph Anthony Fatone Jr.; Chris— Christopher Allen Kirkpatrick; Lance— James Lance Bass; Justin—Justin Timberlake

➤ Fave foods: Justin— cereal; Chris—Mexican; Joey—Italian; J.C.— Chinese; Lance—French toast
➤ J.C.'s dating advice: "Always have gum."
➤ Fun fact: After a breakfast taping at a radio station, Justin's leftover French toast was sold on eBay for $1,025; Lance has since claimed it was his.

Birthday Beat

J.C.: August 8, 1976
Justin: January 31, 1981
Joey: January 28, 1977
Lance: May 4, 1979
Chris: October 17, 1971

*N Sync
7616 Soundland Blvd., #115
Orlando, FL 32809
Official Web site: www.nsync.com

Freddie Prinze Jr.

Cool Credits

➤ Named one of *People*'s 50 Most Beautiful People in the World, 2000
➤ Named one of *Teen People*'s 25 Hottest Stars Under 25
➤ Film: *To Gillian on Her 37th Birthday; The House of Yes; Wing Commander; I Know What You Did Last Summer* and its sequel, *She's All That; Down to You; Boys and Girls; Head over Heels*

Super Stats

➤ Birthplace: Albuquerque, New Mexico
➤ Family: mother, Kathy Cochran, a real estate agent; father, actor-comedian Freddie Prinze, who committed suicide when Freddie was 10 months old

➤ Priorities: avoids the party scene ("I don't fool with drugs.... I would have a father if it wasn't for drugs, bottom line.")
➤ Hobby: collecting comic books; knows the content of every single X-Men comic
➤ Character he relates to most: Spider-Man
➤ Web fact: most-hit actor on Yahoo!
➤ Inspirations: Denzel Washington, Jack Nicholson
➤ Dating: actress Sarah Michelle Gellar
➤ Five most important things in life: "Love. Family. Food. Home. Religion. Not necessarily in that order."

*I*n high school, Freddie felt like an outsider, so he would play-act at being one of his favorite superheroes, the X-Men. Maybe that's why the roles he's chosen have been likable, romantic heroes. In the new comedy-thriller *Head over Heels,* though, he plays a fashion executive who also may be a murderer. But in real life, Freddie has his priorities straight: "Life is not about making dough or how many movies you can make in a year. It's about finding someone that you can share things with."

So You Want to Know—

What's Freddie really like behind the scenes? Costars say he's big-hearted, kind, protective, and considerate. He's also a prankster. Says Rachael Leigh Cook, his costar in *She's All That,* "He was always making faces when I was trying to do a serious scene."

Birthday Beat
March 8, 1976

Freddie Prinze Jr.
c/o Creative Artists Agency
9830 Wilshire Blvd.
Beverly Hills, CA 90212

Christina Ricci

At age 20, Christina is already the veteran of more than a dozen films in 10 years. Not bad for someone who's never had an acting lesson. Whether she's going ghoulish as Wednesday Addams or playing a tortured teen in *The Ice Storm,* Christina can morph into a variety of characters. She's not afraid to tell it like it is, either. "I know I say things all the time and I don't realize how it's going to turn into something else. But I just can't imagine how boring it would be if I had to sit and just say the normal 'Oh yeah, I'm really happy with my life!'"

Super Stats

➤ Birthplace: Santa Monica, California
➤ Family: mother, a therapist turned lawyer, model, and real estate agent; 1 sister, 2 brothers
➤ Learned to read: age 3
➤ Fave book series: C. S. Lewis's *The Chronicles of Narnia*

➤ Pastime: writing. Among her works are diaries, stories, poems, and a script called *Asylum*.

So You Want to Know—

How Christina got her start? A theater critic spotted her at age 8 in a school Christmas pageant and suggested to Christina's parents that she go into acting. A year later she got her first film, *Mermaids,* starring Cher and Winona Ryder, and remains close friends with both actresses.

Cool Credits

➤ Film highlights: *Mermaids, The Addams Family, Addams Family Values, Desert Blue, Buffalo 66, Small Soldiers* (voice-over only), *That Darn Cat, Casper, The Cemetery Club, Now and Then, The Opposite of Sex, The Ice Storm, 200 Cigarettes, Sleepy Hollow*. Next up: *The Man Who Cried* (reuniting with Johnny Depp); will star in and coproduce *Prozac Nation* (with Jason Biggs and Michelle Williams)
➤ Named one of *Teen Movieline*'s 20 Best Actors 25 and Under

Birthday Beat
February 12, 1980

Christina Ricci
c/o International Creative Management
8942 Wilshire Blvd.
Beverly Hills, CA 90211-1934

LeAnn Rimes

From the day she sang "Getting to Know You" at a talent contest when she was 5 years old, LeAnn has set her sights on a career in music. She was barely a teen when she recorded her first major album, *Blue*. LeAnn was the first country singer to win the Grammy for Best New Artist, and her second album, *You Light Up My Life,* debuted at No. 1 on three different *Billboard* charts, making her the first country artist to hold this honor. This teen queen is truly sitting on top of the world!

Birthday Beat

August 28, 1982

So You Want to Know—

What LeAnn's outlook is on stardom? "I don't let it all go to my head. It could all disappear overnight. So I keep reminding myself of that and how hard I've worked to get here."

Cool Credits

➤ Albums: *All That; Blue; You Light Up My Life: Inspirational Songs; The Early Years: Unchained Melody; Sitting on Top of the World; LeAnn Rimes*
➤ Hits: "Blue," "Commitment," "Looking Through Your Eyes," "How Do I Live," "I Need You," "Big Deal," "Written in the Stars" (duet with Elton John)
➤ Grammy Awards, Best New Artist and Best Female Country Vocal (for "Blue"), 1997
➤ 3 Country Music Awards, 1997
➤ TNN Music City Award, 1997
➤ 4 *Billboard* Music Awards, including Artist of the Year, 1997
➤ TV: episodes of *Moesha, Days of Our Lives*; the TV movie "Holiday in Your Heart" (based on her book); host of *Hot 21* and TNN's *Class of 2000*

Super Stats

➤ Full name: Margaret LeAnn Rimes
➤ Birthplace: Jackson, Mississippi
➤ Family: parents, Wilbur and Belinda
➤ Influences: Reba McEntire, Barbra Streisand, Patsy Cline
➤ Pastimes: riding cutting horses, tennis, swimming

LeAnn Rimes
7017 Briarmeadow Dr.
Dallas, TX 75230-5328
or
c/o LeAnn Rimes Fan Club
6060 North Central Expressway, Ste. 816
Dallas, TX 75206
Offical Web site: www.rimestimes.com

Julia Roberts

That face. That smile. It's no secret that Julia can dazzle just about anyone. But Julia is more than just a pretty face; she's a talented, sensitive performer who can bring in the big bucks: Eight of her 24 films have each made more than $100 million. The girl from Smyrna, Georgia—who needed a retainer to fix a space between her two front teeth that had been created by her thumb-sucking—now commands $20 million per film, the first actress ever to do so.

So You Want to Know—

If Julia is fond of practical jokes? A month before shooting began on *Erin Brockovich,* Julia called the director to tell him she was pregnant and that he'd have to shoot around her—a difficult task, considering her character wears tight, form-fitting clothing. Then he looked at the calendar and noticed the date: It was April Fool's!

Birthday Beat
October 28, 1967

Cool Credits

➤ Named one of *People*'s 50 Most Beautiful People in the World, 2000

➤ Ranked at the top of *Forbes* magazine's Power 100 list, above Tom Hanks and Steven Spielberg

➤ Film highlights: *Mystic Pizza, Steel Magnolias, Pretty Woman, The Pelican Brief, Mary Reilly, Michael Collins, My Best Friend's Wedding, Runaway Bride, Notting Hill, Erin Brockovich.* Next up: *The Mexican,* a romantic comedy with Brad Pitt

➤ *Erin Brockovich* was the first movie of 2000 to gross $100 million.

Super Stats

➤ Full name: Julia Fiona Roberts

➤ Birthplace: Smyrna, Georgia

➤ Owns homes in: Taos, New Mexico, and New York City

➤ Family: mother, Betty; father, Walter; brother, actor Eric Roberts; sister, Lisa

➤ Stays in shape with: yoga and 6-mile jogs

➤ Big break: a starring role in *Pretty Woman,* for which she received an Oscar nomination

➤ On her smile: She says it makes her look like "I have a hanger in my mouth."

➤ Dating: actor Benjamin Bratt

Julia Roberts
c/o International Creative Management
8942 Wilshire Blvd.
Beverly Hills, CA 90211
or
6220 Del Valle Dr.
Los Angeles, CA 90048

Alex Rodriguez

Cool Credits

➤ Holds AL record for most single-season home runs (42) by a shortstop, 1998; 1 of only 2 shortstops (with Ernie Banks) to hit 40 or more homers in more than 1 season
➤ 1 of only 2 shortstops (with Cal Ripken) to have 3 .300-average/20-homer seasons
➤ AL All-Star, 1996, 1997, 1998
➤ *Players Choice* AL Player of the Year, 1998
➤ Gatorade's National Student Athlete of the Year in baseball, 1993
➤ 2 Silver Slugger Awards

Super Stats

➤ Team: Seattle Mariners (shortstop)
➤ Full name: Alexander Emmanuel Rodriguez
➤ Nickname: A-Rod
➤ Height: 6'3"
➤ Weight: 210
➤ Birthplace: New York City
➤ Current residence: Miami, Florida
➤ Launched the educational program Grand Slam for Kids
➤ Childhood idol: Cal Ripken (They are now good friends, and Alex often visits Cal at his Maryland home to shoot hoops.)

So You Want to Know—

How Alex maintains his athletic build? He avoids junk food, follows an intense workout regimen, and keeps a positive attitude. "We get stereotyped that we're not in good shape, that we're not athletes. Believe me, if you play second base, shortstop, or centerfield, you had better be in good shape. My philosophy is, the more I enhance myself, the better."

*F*ew baseball players have dominated the league at such a young age as Alex has. In 1998, he became the third player in history to join the 40/40 club (40 homers and 40 steals in a season). Alex credits much of his success to his mother. She scraped together enough money to send him to high school at the Westminster Academy, the best baseball program in the U.S., where his teacher was the legendary coach Rich Hofman.

Birthday Beat
July 27, 1975

Alex Rodriguez
c/o Seattle Mariners
P.O. Box 4100
Seattle, WA 98104

Rebecca Romijn-Stamos

Red-hot Rebecca Romijn-Stamos (that's roh-MAYN) is well aware of her status as both a model *and* a role model. "Nobody is perfect, myself included, and every model you have ever seen. You have to let kids know that." After a year in college, she signed with an agency and modeled in Paris for two years. The host of MTV's *House of Style* is now flexing her acting muscles as the blue-skinned, shape-shifting villain Mystique in this summer's x-citing *X-Men* movie.

So You Want to Know—
What Rebecca thinks her most beguiling feature is? Her oddball sense of humor. When asked why she always seems to play gross girls—she was Jerry's messy girlfriend on *Seinfeld* and the bearded lady in the film *Dirty Work*—she replies, "Because that's the point. I don't want to play a model."

Cool Credits

➤ Modeling contracts: Pantene, Tommy Hilfiger, Victoria's Secret
➤ Magazine covers: *Elle, GQ, Sports Illustrated*'s 1999 Swimsuit Issue
➤ Host of MTV's *House of Style* since 1998
➤ Film: *Dirty Work, Austin Powers: The Spy Who Shagged Me, X-Men*
➤ TV: recurring role on *Just Shoot Me*; appeared on *Friends, Seinfeld*
➤ Named one of *People*'s 50 Most Beautiful People in the World, 1999

Super Stats

➤ Height: 5'11"
➤ Birthplace: Berkeley, California
➤ Current residences: Los Angeles, New York City, Paris
➤ Nickname while growing up: the Jolly Blonde Giant
➤ Family: married to actor John Stamos
➤ Secret talent: making dollhouses
➤ Biggest regret: says she once cut her hair super-short in Paris and cried for 3 years straight
➤ Fave artists: Nina Simone, Radiohead, the Beastie Boys

Birthday Beat

November 6, 1972

Rebecca Romijn-Stamos
c/o MTV's House of Style
1515 Broadway
New York, NY 10036
or
c/o IMG Models
304 Park Ave. South, Penthouse North
New York, NY 10010

Pete Sampras

ith his easygoing nature, flawless technique, and killer serve, no wonder Pete was the No. 1 player in the world for six straight years, from 1993 through 1998. Although he had a couple of setbacks in 1999—an injury caused him to drop from the No. 1 spot, and he lost to Andre Agassi in the Australian Open, where he tore a hip muscle—Pete is now back in the game. Experts say that when he is in top form, he is still the best player in the world.

Super Stats

➤ Height: 6'1"
➤ Weight: 170
➤ Birthplace: Washington, D.C.
➤ Current residence: Tampa, Florida
➤ Family: parents, Georgia and Sam; brother, Gus; sisters, Stella and Marion
➤ Began playing tennis at: age 7
➤ Fave book: *Catcher in the Rye*
➤ Fave artists: U2, Led Zeppelin

➤ Charities: Aces for Charity (which he started to create cancer awareness), the Tim and Tom Gullikson Foundation (Tim was Pete's coach before he died of cancer.)

Cool Credits

➤ Has won 12 Grand Slam titles: Wimbledon, 1993, 1994, 1995, 1997, 1998, 1999; U.S. Open, 1990, 1993, 1995, 1996; Australian Open, 1994, 1997

➤ French Open semi-finalist, 1996
➤ First to score more than 1,000 aces in a single season, 1993
➤ IBM/ATP World Champion, 1991
➤ Youngest player to win the U.S. Open, 1990
➤ 1 of only 2 players (with Bjorn Borg) to win at least 1 Grand Slam title in 5 consecutive years

Birthday Beat
August 12, 1971

So You Want to Know—
What Pete learned from his loss to Agassi? "After Australia, I realized that I needed to pay more attention to my physical training," he has said. "I have to take the time to make sure that I'm ready to play."

Pete Sampras
6352 Maclaurin Dr.
Tampa, FL 33647-1164
Official Web site: www.sampras.com

Adam Sandler

From his earliest days, Adam never wanted to be anything but a comedian. He was a class clown starting in grammar school, and attended college while juggling a standup comedy career. In his freshman year, he had a recurring role on *The Cosby Show,* playing Theo's pal Smitty. His credentials also include writing and producing, and with box office hits such as *The Waterboy* and *Big Daddy* under his belt, there's no stopping this wild and crazy guy!

■ ■ ■ ■ ■ ■ ■ ■ ■ ■ ■ ■ ■ ■ ■ ■

Cool Credits

➤ Film: *Airheads, Mixed Nuts, Billy Madison* (also screenwriter), *Happy Gilmore* (also screenwriter), *Bulletproof, The Wedding Singer, The Waterboy, Dirty Work, Big Daddy, Little Nicky* (in which he costars with Beefy, a talking bulldog, and plays the son of the Devil)
➤ Nominated for a Grammy for his debut comedy album, *They're All Gonna Laugh at You*

➤ TV: *The Cosby Show, Saturday Night Live, Remote Control*

Super Stats

➤ Birthplace: Brooklyn, New York
➤ Raised in: New Hampshire
➤ Education: graduated from New York University with a degree in fine arts

So You Want to Know—

How Adam got his start? He was performing at the Improv in Los Angeles when Dennis Miller, an alumnus of *Saturday Night Live,* caught his act. Adam was quickly hired as an *SNL* writer and cast member, and a year later he had captured the hearts of TV viewers with his "Opera Man" and "Canteen Boy" characters.

Adam Sandler
9701 Wilshire Blvd., 10th Floor
Beverly Hills, CA 90212

Britney Spears

*E*ver since she was a little girl, Britney has been dancing and putting on shows. With her take-charge moves and catchy tunes, she's raised girl power to a higher level. The former *Mickey Mouse Club* member is a down-to-earth girl with a big heart and just a touch of the wild side. With the release of her second album, a new memoir, and a budding acting career, Britney's not about to let her leagues of fans down. "I'm living proof that you can succeed, no matter where you're from or how little you have."

So You Want to Know—

How Britney deals with stress? Besides writing in a prayer journal, she and her assistant play a game in which Britney pretends to be someone else—anyone from Ashley Judd to Lenny Kravitz.

Cool Credits

➤ Albums: *…Baby One More Time* (which sold 9 million copies), *Oops!… I Did It Again*
➤ First debut artist to hit No. 1 on both the *Billboard* album chart and *Billboard*'s Hot 100 in the same week (with *…Baby One More Time*)
➤ Memoir: *Britney Spears' Heart to Heart,* cowritten with her mother
➤ TV: *Sabrina the Teenage Witch*
➤ Film: *Jack of All Trades* (upcoming)
➤ Named one of *Teen People*'s 25 Hottest Stars Under 25

Super Stats

➤ Birthplace: Kentwood, Louisiana
➤ Family: mother, Lynne, a teacher; father, Jamie, a building contractor; sister, Jamie Lynne; brother, Bryan
➤ Fave CD: Macy Gray's *On How Life Is*
➤ Pet: a Yorkshire terrier puppy named Baby
➤ Loves: romance novels
➤ What's inside her tour bus: a tanning bed and a bedroom with lace, candles, and a queen-size bed with a lavender comforter and pillows that say "Britney"
➤ Friends: Christina Aguilera and Justin Timberlake
➤ Bad habit: bites her nails

Birthday Beat

December 2, 1981

• •

Britney Spears
137 W. 25th St.
New York, NY 10001

• •

Sheryl Swoopes

▼▼▼▼▼▼▼▼▼▼▼▼▼▼▼▼▼▼

When she was a kid, Sheryl wanted to play basketball, but her brothers always played rough on the court. Determined to succeed, Sheryl plunged in and proved she's definitely got game. The WNBA signed her in 1997, and she proceeded to lead the Comets to back-to-back championship rings. Sheryl is the first female athlete to have a shoe named after her, the Air Swoopes.

So You Want to Know—
What Sheryl's reaction was when she learned Nike wanted to name a shoe after her? "I was speechless. I cried. I bawled. At first I thought they were joking…. I was just out of it. I thought I was dreaming."

Cool Credits

➤ Led the Comets to 2 WNBA championship rings, 1997, 1998
➤ All-WNBA First Team, 1998
➤ Signed by the WNBA and joined the Comets in 1997
➤ Gold medal, U.S. Women's Olympic Team, 1996
➤ Member, undefeated Women's National Team, which had a 52–0 record in 1995–96
➤ National Player of the Year, 1993
➤ NCAA Final Four MVP, 1993
➤ Ranked second in nation with 28.1 points per game, 1992, 1993

Super Stats

➤ Team: Houston Comets (forward)
➤ Full name: Sheryl Denise Swoopes
➤ Height: 6'0"
➤ Weight: 145
➤ Hometown: Brownfield, Texas
➤ Education: Texas Tech, where she broke Bill Walton's record for most points ever scored in a Division I NCAA championship game
➤ Family: married her high school sweetheart, Eric Jackson; son, Jordan
➤ Goal: to pursue sports broadcasting after her basketball career is over
➤ Fave foods: Mexican, pralines 'n' cream ice cream

Birthday Beat

March 25, 1971

Sheryl Swoopes
c/o Houston Comets
2 Greenway Plaza, Ste. 400
Houston, TX 77046

Usher

*T*he utter truth about Usher? He has got charisma with a capital C. His smooth vocals, adorable baby face, and electric moves make him the king of hip-hop soul. Raised in Tennessee, where he sang in the church choir, Usher's family moved to Atlanta when he was 12. He appeared in talent shows, caught the eye of a record executive, and recorded his first album by age 16. This talented musician also is an up-and-coming actor and record producer. Is there anything he *can't* do?

Birthday Beat
October 14, 1978

So You Want to Know—
What TV show Usher would like to appear on? "I'd choose *Lifestyles of the Rich and Famous* because then I could show off my houses."

Cool Credits

➤ Hit singles: "Let's Straighten It Out" (duet with Monica), "Think of You," "You Make Me Wanna" (which stayed at the top of the charts for 11 weeks), "Nice and Slow," "My Way"
➤ Albums: *Usher, My Way*
➤ Film: *The Faculty, She's All That, Light It Up, Texas Rangers.* Next up: *Facade* (as writer and producer)
➤ TV: *Moesha, The Bold and the Beautiful,* Disney's *Geppetto* (starring Drew Carey)

Super Stats

➤ Full name: Usher Raymond IV
➤ Birthplace: Dallas, Texas
➤ Raised in: Chattanooga, Tennessee

➤ Current residence: Atlanta, Georgia
➤ Family: mother, Jonetta Patton, his manager; younger brother, James
➤ Stays healthy by: drinking a mixture of cranberry and orange juice in the morning
➤ Person he trusts most on earth: his mom
➤ His own record label: Us Records
➤ Fave breakfast: scrambled egg whites, oatmeal, green tea
➤ Fave snacks: hot dogs and ice cream
➤ What he looks for in a girl: confidence, and the way she dresses and walks
➤ One of his worst moments: when a guy he considered a close friend told Usher he would never act

Usher Raymond
808 Ridgeley
Los Angeles, CA 90038

Denzel Washington

Mega-talented Denzel has earned the respect of audiences and actors, who call him a generous and gracious costar. He's also a dedicated one: Denzel spent 16 months of up to 4-hour-a-day workouts preparing for the role of boxer Rubin

"Hurricane" Carter. Above all, he values the importance of family. "I had a lot of love at home and some luck…. Some people don't have enough [love] at home that might make them think twice about things."

So You Want to Know—

Just how important family is to Denzel? He often has it written into his film contracts that he have weekends off to fly home. "My career has been enhanced by family, stability, having birthday parties. If I didn't have a family, what would I be doing this weekend?"

Cool Credits

➤ Film: *A Soldier's Story, The Mighty Quinn, Cry Freedom, Mo' Better Blues, The Pelican Brief, Malcolm X, Courage Under Fire, The Preacher's Wife, Crimson Tide, Devil in a Blue Dress, Mississippi Masala, Philadelphia, He Got Game, The Bone Collector, The Hurricane*
➤ TV: *St. Elsewhere*, the TV movies *Flesh and Blood* and *Wilma*, the cable documentary *Hank Aaron: Chasing the Dream* (executive producer)
➤ Stage: *Ceremonies in Dark Old Men, Othello, A Soldier's Play*
➤ Golden Globe, Best Actor in a Drama, *The Hurricane*, 2000
➤ NAACP Image Awards for *Mississippi Masala*, 1993; *The Hurricane*, 2000

➤ Academy Award, Best Supporting Actor, *Glory*, 1990

Super Stats

➤ Birthplace: Mount Vernon, New York
➤ Current residence: Beverly Hills, California
➤ Family: wife, singer-pianist Pauletta Pearson; children, John David, Katia, twins Malcolm and Olivia; mother, Lennis; father, Denzel, was a Pentecostal preacher
➤ Education: Fordham University, where he majored in pre-med, switching to journalism and drama; American Conservatory Theater
➤ Pastime: coaching his kids' basketball teams
➤ Fave charity: the Nelson Mandela Children's Fund

Denzel Washington
4701 Sancola
Toluca Lake, CA 91602

Serena Williams

▼▼▼▼▼▼▼▼▼▼▼▼▼▼▼▼▼▼▼

She often shares the tennis spotlight with her older sister, Venus, but Serena is a rising star in her own right. After going pro only a year before, she won five titles in 1999 alone, including the U.S. Open. In her first Grand Slam victory, Serena upset Lindsay Davenport, Monica Seles, and top-seeded Martina Hingis. This braided, beaded dynamo will continue to be a powerful presence on the courts in the years to come.

So You Want to Know—

How long it takes to do all those beads? An appointment at the hair salon can take up to four hours to change Serena's braids and beads.

Cool Credits

➤ Won the U.S. Open Women's Singles title and (with Venus) the Women's Doubles title, 1999
➤ With Venus, won the French Open Women's Doubles tournament, 1999
➤ Won 2 mixed-doubles tournaments with partner Max Mirnyi in 1998, her first professional year—Wimbledon and the U.S. Open
➤ Lowest seeded player, and the only black player, in the Open era to win at Flushing Meadows (where the U.S. Open is played)
➤ Serena and Venus are the first sisters in professional tennis history to win singles titles in the same week.

Super Stats

➤ Height: 5'10"
➤ Birthplace: Saginaw, Michigan
➤ Current residence: Palm Beach Gardens, Florida
➤ Nickname: the Steamroller
➤ Family: sisters, Venus, Yetunde, Isha, Lyndrea; father, Richard, coaches both Serena and Venus; mother, Oracene (Brandi)
➤ Turned pro: 1998
➤ Plays: right-handed (two-handed backhand)
➤ Likes: playing on hard courts, which makes her a formidable opponent year-round
➤ Fave singer: Vanilla Ice (!)

Birthday Beat
September 26, 1981

Serena Williams
c/o Sanex WTA Tour
1266 E. Main St., 4th Floor
Stamford, CT 06902

Tiger Woods

Has he ever been seen *without* a golf club in his hand? At age 2, Tiger appeared on *The Mike Douglas Show* and putted with Bob Hope. He was featured in *Golf Digest* at 5 years of age, turned pro at age 20, and won the most prestigious tourna-ment, the Masters, just two years later. Although he's already established himself as a living golf legend, he still has many more years to play. But if Tiger's amazing win

at the 2000 U.S. Open is any indication, he may become the greatest golfer in history.

Birthday Beat
December 30, 1975

Cool Credits

➤ 12 PGA Tour victories in 1999 and 2000: 1999 Buick Invitational, 1999 Memorial, 1999 Western Open, 1999 PGA Championship, 1999 World Series of Golf, 1999 National Car Rental Golf Classic, 1999 Tour Championship, 1999 World Golf Championship, 2000 Mercedes Championship, 2000 AT&T Pebble Beach National Pro-AM, 2000 Bay Hill Invitational Classic, 2000 U.S. Open
➤ Tied Ben Hogan with 6 consecutive PGA championships
➤ Led the PGA money list in 1997
➤ PGA Player of the Year, 1997
➤ PGA Rookie of the Year, 1996

Super Stats

➤ Real name: Eldrick Woods
➤ Height: 6'2"
➤ Birthplace: Cypress, California
➤ Current residence: Orlando, Florida
➤ Family: father, Earl, is a retired lieutenant colonel in the U.S. Army; mother, Kultida, is a native of Thailand
➤ Education: attended Stanford University

So You Want to Know—

Where Tiger got his name? He was named after Vuong Dang Phong, a Vietnamese soldier and friend of his father. Earl had given Vuong Dang the nickname Tiger, then passed it on to his only son.

Tiger Woods
4281 Katella Ave., #111
Los Alamitos, CA 90720-3541

Photo Credits

Cover:

Interior: